D1126407

THOREAU
ON MAN &
NATURE

PETER PAUPER PRESS

MOUNT VERNON · NEW YORK

THOREAU ON MAN
AND NATURE

A COMPILATION BY
ARTHUR G. VOLKMAN
FROM THE WRITINGS
OF HENRY D. THOREAU

1. ALMA NATURA

℃ Every leaf and twig was this morning covered with a sparkling ice armor; even the grasses in exposed fields were hung with innumerable diamond pendants, which jingled merrily when brushed by the foot of the traveler. It was literally the wreck of jewels and the crash of gems. . . . Such is beauty ever —

neither here nor there, now nor then — neither in Rome nor in Athens, but wherever there is a soul to admire. If I seek her elsewhere because I do not find her at home, my search will prove a fruitless one.

❦ The thin snow now driving from the north and lodging on my coat consists of those beautiful star crystals, not cottony and chubby spokes, but thick and partly transparent crystals. They are about a tenth of an inch in diameter, perfect little wheels with six spokes without a tire, or rather with six perfect little leaflets, fern-like, with a distinct straight and slender midrib, raying from the center. . . . How full of the creative genius is the air in which they are generated. I should hardly admire more if real stars fell and lodged on my coat.

❦ We are rained and snowed on with gems. What a world we live in! Where are the jewelers' shops? There is nothing handsomer than a snowflake and dewdrop. I may say that the maker of the world exhausts his skill with each snowflake and dewdrop he sends down. We think that the one mechanically coheres and that the other simply flows together and falls, but in truth they are the product of *enthusiasm,* the children of an ecstasy, finished with the artist's utmost skill.

❡ This restless and now swollen stream has burst its icy fetters, and as I stand looking up it westward for half a mile, where it winds slightly under a high bank, its surface is lit up here and there with a fine-grained silvery sparkle which makes the river appear something celestial—more than a terrestrial river—which might have suggested that which surrounded the shield of Homer. If rivers come out of their icy prison thus bright and immortal, shall not I too resume my spring life with joy and hope? Have I no hopes to sparkle on the surface of life's current?

❡ I have an appointment with spring. She comes to the window to wake me, and I go forth an hour or two earlier than usual. Though as yet the trill of the chip-bird is not heard — added — like the sparkling bead which bursts on bottled cider or ale. When we wake indeed, with a double awakening — not only from our ordinary nocturnal slumbers, but from our diurnal—we burst through the thallus of our ordinary life with a proper exciple, we wake with emphasis.

❡ The grass flames up on the hillsides like a spring fire — as if the earth sent forth an inward heat to greet the returning sun; not yellow but green is the color of its flame; — the symbol of perpetual youth, the grass-blade, like a long green ribbon, streams from the sod into the summer, checked indeed by the frost, but anon pushing on again, lifting its spear of last year's hay with a fresh life below. It grows as steadily as the rill oozes out of the ground. It is almost identical with that, for in the growing days of June, when the rills are dry, the grass blades are their channels, and from year to year the herds drink at this perennial green stream and the mower draws from it betimes their winter supply.

ℂ These motions everywhere in nature must surely be the circulations of God. The flowing sail, the running stream, the waving tree, the roving wind — whence else their infinite health and freedom. I can see nothing so proper and holy as unrelaxed play and frolic in this bower God has built for us. The suspicion of sin never comes to this thought. Oh, if men felt this they would never build temples even of marble or diamond, but it would be sacrilege and prophane, but disport them forever in this paradise.

ℂ I saw a distant river by moonlight, making no noise, yet flowing, as by day, still to the sea, like melted silver reflecting the moonlight. Far away it lay encircling the earth. How far away it may look in the night, and even from a low hill how miles away down the valley. As far off as paradise and the delectable country. There is a certain glory attends on water by night. By it the heavens are related to the earth, undistinguishable from a sky beneath you.

℄ It is a luxury to muse by a well-side in the sunshine of a September afternoon — to cuddle down under a gray stone, and hearken to the siren song of the cricket. Day and night seem henceforth but accidents, and the time is always a still eventide, and as the close of a happy day. Parched fields and mulleins gilded with the slanting rays are my diet. I know of no word so fit to express this disposition of Nature as Alma Natura.

℄ October is the month for painted leaves. Their rich glow now flashes round the world. As fruits and leaves and the day itself acquire a bright tint just before they fall, so the year near its setting. October is its sunset sky; November the later twilight.

℄ We had a remarkable sunset one day last November. I was walking in a meadow, the source of a small brook, when the sun at last, just before setting, after a cold gray day, reached a clear stratum in the horizon, and the softest brightest sunlight fell on the dry

9

grass and on the stems of the trees in the op-
posite horizon and on the leaves of the shrub-
oaks on the hill-side, while our shadows
stretched long over the meadow eastward, as
if we were the only motes in its beams. It was
such a light as we could not have imagined
a moment before, and the air also was so
warm and serene that nothing was wanting to
make a paradise of that meadow. When we
reflected that this was not a solitary phe-
nomenon, never to happen again, but that it
would happen forever and ever an infinite
number of evenings, and cheer and reassure
the latest child that walked there, it was more
glorious still.

ℂ Evening. Though the sun set a quarter of
an hour ago, his rays are still visible, darting
half-way to the zenith. That glowing morrow
in the west flashes on me like a faint presenti-
ment of morning when I am falling asleep. A
dull mist comes rolling from the west, as if it
were the dust which day has raised. A column
of smoke is rising from the woods yonder, to
uphold heaven's roof till the light comes
again. The landscape, by its patient resting
there, teaches me that all good remains with
him that waiteth, and that I shall sooner over-
take the dawn by remaining here, than by
hurrying over the hills of the west.

2. OF ASPIRATION

℀ Every man is the builder of a temple, called his body, to the God he worships, after a style purely his own, nor can he get off by hammering marble instead. We are all sculptors and painters, and our material is our own flesh and blood and bones. Any nobleness begins at once to refine a man's features, any meanness or sensuality to imbrute them.

❦ Each reaching and aspiration is an instinct with which all nature consists and cooperates and therefore it is not in vain. But alas! each relaxing and desperation is an instinct too.

❦ I know of no more encouraging fact than the unquestionable ability of man to elevate his life by a conscious endeavor.

❦ True a man cannot lift himself by his own waistbands, because he cannot get out of himself; but he can expand himself (which is better, there is no up nor down in nature), and so split his waistbands, being already within himself.

❦ Shall a man go and hang himself because he belongs to the race of pygmies, and not be the biggest pygmy that he can? Let every man mind his own business, and endeavor to be what he was made.

❦ Do a little more of that work which you had sometime confessed to be good, which you feel that society and your justest judge rightly demands of you. Do what you reprove yourself for not doing. Know that you are neither satisfied nor dissatisfied with yourself without reason. Let me say to you and to myself in one breath, Cultivate the tree which you have found to bear fruit in your soil.

❧ We know not yet what we have done, still less what we are doing. Wait till evening and other parts of our day's work will shine than we had thought at noon, and we shall discover the real purport of our toil.

❧ In the long run men hit only what they aim at. Therefore, though they should fail immediately, they had better aim at something high.

❧ How many a poor immortal soul have I met well nigh crushed and smothered under its load, creeping down the road of life, pushing before it a barn seventy-five feet by forty, its Augean stables never cleansed, and one hundred acres of land, tillage, mowing, pasture, and wood-lot! The portionless, who struggle with no such unnecessary inherited encumbrances, find it labor enough to subdue and cultivate a few cubic feet of flesh.

❧ Be resolutely and faithfully what you are, be humbly what you aspire to be. Be sure you give men the best of your wares, though they be poor enough, and the gods will help you to lay up a better store for the future.

❧ Give me the old familiar world, post-office and all, with this ever new self, with this infinite expectation and faith, which does not know when it is beaten.

❡ I have aspired to practice in succession all the honest arts of life, that I may gather all their fruits. But then, if you are intemperate, if you toil to raise an unnecessary amount of corn, even the large crop of wheat becomes as a small crop of chaff.

❡ I wish to live ever as to derive my satisfactions and inspirations from the commonest events, every-day phenomena, so that what my senses hourly perceive, my daily walk, the conversation of my neighbors, may inspire me, and I may dream of no heaven but that which lies about me.

❡ Beware of all enterprises that require new clothes, and not rather a new wearer of clothes. If there is not a new man, how can the new clothes be made to fit? If you have any enterprise before you, try it in your old clothes.

❡ So we saunter toward the Holy Land, till one day the sun shall shine more brightly than ever he has done, shall perchance shine into our minds and hearts, and light up our whole lives with a great awakening light, as warm and serene and golden as on a bank-side in autumn.

3. ORIENTATION

❡ Not till we are lost, in other words, not till we have lost the world, do we begin to find ourselves, and realize where we are and the infinite extent of our relations.

❡ See what a life the gods have given us, set round with pain and pleasure. It is too strange for sorrow! it is too strange for joy. One while it looks as shallow, though as intricate as a Cretan labyrinth, and again it is a path-less depth.

❦ With thinking we may be beside ourselves in a sane sense. By a conscious effort of the mind we can stand aloof from actions and their consequences; and all things, good and bad, go by like a torrent.

❦ If for a moment we make way with our petty selves, wish no ill to anything, appre-hend no ill, cease to be but the crystal which reflects a ray—what shall we not reflect! What a universe will appear crystallized and radiant around us!

❦ It is never too late to give up our preju-dices. No way of thinking or doing, however ancient, can be trusted without proof. What everybody echoes or in silence passes by as true today may turn out to be falsehood to-morrow, mere smoke of opinion, which some had trusted for a cloud that would sprinkle fertilizing rain on their fields. What old people say you cannot do, you try and find that you can. Old deeds for old people, and new deeds for new.

❦ Most men, even in this comparatively free country, through mere ignorance and mis-take, are so occupied with the factitious cares and superfluously coarse labors of life that its finer fruits cannot be plucked by them. Their fingers, from excessive toil, are too clumsy and tremble too much for that. Actually, the laboring man has not leisure for a true integrity day by day; he cannot afford to sustain the manliest relations to men; his labor would be depreciated in the market. He has no time to be anything but a machine.

℃ A single gentle rain makes the grass many shades greener. So our prospects brighten on the influx of better thoughts. We should be blessed if we lived in the present always, and took advantage of every accident that befell us, like the grass which confesses the influence of the slightest dew that falls on it.

℃ A great nature will not consider its sins as its own, but be more absorbed in the prospect of that valor and virtue for the future which is more properly it, than in the improper actions which, by being sins, discover themselves to be not it.

℃ In the spring I burned over a hundred acres till the earth was sere and black, and by midsummer this space was clad in a fresher and more luxuriant green than the surrounding even. Shall man then despair? Is he not a sproutland too, after never so many searings and witherings?

❡ The skeleton which at first sight excites only a shudder in all mortals becomes at last not only a pure but suggestive and pleasing object to science. The more we know of it, the less we associate it with any goblin of our imaginations. The longer we keep it, the less likely it is that any such will come to claim it. We discover that the only spirit which haunts it is a universal intelligence which has created it in harmony with all nature. Science never saw a ghost, nor does it look for any, but it sees everywhere the traces, and it is itself the agent, of a Universal Intelligence.

❡ Knowledge does not come to us by details, but in flashes of light from heaven.

❡ In a pleasant spring morning all men's sins are forgiven. Through our own recovered innocence we discern the innocence of our neighbors.

❡ What an admirable training is science for the more active warfare of life. Indeed, the unchallenged bravery, which these studies imply, is far more impressive than the trumpeted valor of the warrior. Science is always brave, for to know, is to know good; doubt and danger quail before her eye. But cowardice is unscientific; for there cannot be a science of ignorance.

❦ I do not know how to distinguish between our waking life and a dream. Are we not always living the life that we imagine we are?

❦ Misfortunes occur only when a man is false to his Genius. Every human being is the artificer of his own fate in these respects. The well have no time to be sick. Events, circumstances, etc., have their origin in ourselves. They spring from seeds which we have sown.

❦ Explore your own higher altitudes. . . . Nay be a Columbus to whole new continents and worlds within you, opening new channels, not of trade but of thought. Every man is the lord of a realm beside which the earthly empire of the Czar is but a petty state, a hummock left by the ice. Yet some can be patriotic who have no *self* respect, and sacrifice the greater to the less. They love the soil which makes their graves, but have no sympathy with the spirit which may still animate their clay.

❦ It is well to have some water in your neighborhood, to give buoyancy to and float the earth. One value even of the smallest well is, that when you look into it you see that earth is not continent but insular. This is as important as that it keep butter cool.

4. GENERATION

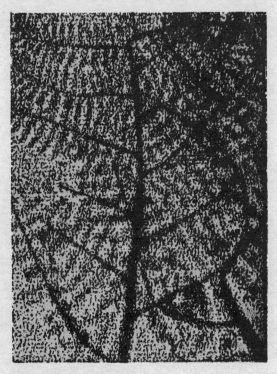

℃ Man is the artificer of his own happiness. Let him beware how he complains of the disposition of circumstances, for it is his own disposition he blames. If this is sour, or that rough, or the other steep, let him think if it be not his work. If his look curdles all hearts, let him not complain of a sour reception; if he hobbles in his gait, let him not grumble at the roughness of the way; if he is weak in the knees, let him not call the hill steep.

℃ Our least deed, like the young of the land crab, wends its way to the sea of cause and effect as soon as born, and makes a drop there to eternity.

℃ The generative energy, which when we are loose, dissipates and makes us unclean, when we are continent invigorates and inspires us. Chastity is the flowering of man; and what are called Genius, Heroism, Holiness, and the like, are but various fruits which succeed it. Man flows at once to God when the channel of purity is open. By turns our purity inspires and our impurity casts us down. He is blessed who is assured that the animal is dying out in him day by day and the divine being established.

℃ It is hard to be a good citizen of the world in any great sense; but if we render no interest or increase to mankind out of that talent God gave us, we can at least preserve the principle unimpaired. One would like to be making large dividends to society out of that deposit capital in us, but he does well for the most part if he proves a secure investment only without adding to the stock.

❡ I came into this world, not chiefly to make this a good place to live in, but to live in it, be it good or bad. A man has not everything to do, but something; and because he cannot do *everything,* it is not necessary that he should do *something* wrong.

❡ To affect the quality of the day, that is the highest of the arts.

❡ In any weather, at any hour of the day or night, I have been anxious to improve the nick of time, and notch it on my stick too; to stand on the meeting of two eternities, the past and future, which is precisely the present moment; to toe that line.

❡ If I would preserve my relation to nature, I must make my life more moral, more pure and innocent. The problem is so precise and simple as a mathematical one. I must not live loosely, but more and more continently.

❡ How watchful we must be to keep the crystal well that we were made, clear! — that it be not made turbid by our contact with the world, so that it will not reflect objects. What other liberty is there worth having, if we have not freedom and peace in our minds — if our inmost and most private man is but a sour and turbid pool?

❡ To him whose elastic and vigorous thought keeps pace with the sun, the day is a perpetual morning. It matters not what the clocks say or the attitudes and labors of men. Morning is when I am awake and there is a dawn in me.

❡ We are double-edged blades, and every time we whet our virtue the return stroke strops our vice.

❡ If you would avoid uncleanness and all the sins, work earnestly, though it be at cleaning a stable.

❡ As for conforming outwardly, and living your own life inwardly, I do not think much of that. When you get God to pulling one way, and the devil the other, each having his feet well braced — to say nothing of the conscience sawing transversely—almost any timber will give way.

❡ I have no time to read newspapers. If you chance to live and move and have your being in that thin stratum in which the events which make the news transpire — thinner than the paper on which it is printed — then these things will fill the world for you; but if you soar above or dive below that plane, you cannot remember nor be reminded of them.

❡ What a man thinks of himself, that is which determines, or rather indicates, his fate.

❦ The fate of the country does not depend on how you vote at the polls — the worst man is as strong as the best at that game; it does not depend on what kind of paper you drop into the ballot-box once a year, but on what kind of man you drop from your chamber into the street every morning.

❦ However mean your life is, meet it and live; do not shun it and call it hard names. It is not so bad as you are. It looks poorest when you are richest. The fault-finder will find faults even in paradise. Love your life, poor as it is. You may perchance have some pleasant, thrilling, glorious hours, even in a poorhouse.

❦ The millions are awake enough for physical labor; but only one in a million is awake enough for effective intellectual exertion, only one in a hundred millions to a poetic or divine life. To be awake is to be alive. I have never yet met a man who was quite awake. How could I have looked him in the face?

❦ Could a greater miracle take place than for us to look through each other's eyes for an instant? We should live in all the ages of the world in an hour; ay, in all the worlds of the ages. History, Poetry, Mythology!—I know of no reading of another's experience so startling and informing as this would be.

❡ Cultivate poverty like sage, like a garden herb. Do not trouble yourself to get new things, whether clothes or friends. That is dissipation. Turn the old, return to them. Things do not change; we change. If I were confined to a corner in a garret all my days, like a spider, the world would be just as large to me while I had my thoughts.

❡ You conquer fate by thought.

❡ It would be worth the while to ask ourselves weekly, Is our life innocent enough? Do we live *inhumanely,* toward man or beast, in thought or act? To be serene and successful we must be at one with the universe. The least conscious and needless injury inflicted on any creature is to its extent a suicide. What peace — or life — can a murderer have?

❡ I would fain improve every opportunity to wonder and worship, as a sunflower welcomes the light. The more thrilling, wonderful, divine objects I behold in a day, the more expanded and immortal I become. If a stone appeals to me and elevates me, tells me how many miles I have come, how many remain to travel — and the more, the better — reveals the future to me in some measure, it is a matter of private rejoicing.

5. MIND PRINTS

❦ I am grateful for what I am and have. My thanksgiving is perpetual. It is surprising how contented one can be with nothing definite — only a sense of existence. My breath is sweet to me. O how I laugh when I think of my vague indefinite riches. No run on my bank can drain it, for my wealth is not possession but enjoyment.

❡ What you call bareness and poverty is to me simplicity. God could not be unkind to me if he should try. I have never got over my surprise that I should have been born into the most estimable place in all the world, and in the very nick of time, too.

❡ In proportion as he simplifies his life, the laws of the universe will appear less complex, and solitude will not be solitude, nor poverty poverty, nor weakness weakness.

❡ The setting sun is reflected from the windows of the almshouse as brightly as from the rich man's house. The snow melts before its door as early in the spring. I do not see but a quiet mind may live as contentedly there, and have as cheering thoughts as anywhere, and, indeed, the town's poor seem to live the most independent lives of any. They are simply great enough to receive without misgiving.

❡Our life is frittered away by detail. An honest man had hardly need to count more than his ten fingers, or in extreme cases he may add his ten toes, and lump the rest. Simplicity, simplicity, simplicity. I say, let your affairs be as two or three, and not a hundred or a thousand; instead of a million count half a dozen, and keep your accounts on your thumb-nail.

℃ By poverty, i.e., simplicity of life and fewness of incidents, I am solidified and crystallized, as a vapor or liquid by cold. It is a singular concentration of strength and energy and flavor. Chastity is perpetual acquaintance with the All.

℃ Most of the luxuries, and many of the so-called comforts of life, are not only not indispensable, but positive hindrances to the elevation of mankind. With respect to luxuries and comforts, the wisest have ever lived a more simple and meager life than the poor.

℃ There is no odor so bad as that which arises from goodness tainted. It is human, it is divine, carrion. If I knew for a certainty that a man was coming to my house with the conscious design of doing me good, I should run for my life.

℃ Everyone who deserves to be regarded as higher than the brute may be supposed to have an earnest purpose, to accomplish which is the object of his existence; and this is at once his work and his supremest pleasure; and for diversion and relaxation, for suggestion and education and strength, there is offered the never-failing amusement of getting a living — never-failing, I mean, when temperately indulged in.

❧ No humane being, past the thoughtless age of boyhood, will wantonly murder any creature which holds its life by the same tenure that he does.

❧ Routine is a ground to stand on, a wall to retreat to; we cannot draw on our boots without bracing ourselves against it. Our health requires that we should recline on it from time to time. Our weakness wants it, but our strength uses it. Good for the body is the work of the body, good for the soul the work of the soul, and good for either the work of the other.

❧ Our thoughts are the epochs of our lives; all else is but as a journal of the winds that blew while we were here.

❧ When the heavens are obscured to us, and nothing noble or heroic appears, but we are oppressed by imperfection and shortcoming on all hands, we are apt to suck our thumbs and decry our fates. As if nothing was to be done in cloudy weather, or, if heaven were not accessible by the upper road, men would not find a lower. There are two ways to victory — to strive bravely, or to yield. How much pain the last will save us we have not yet learned.

6. OF COURAGE

❦ Cowards would not have victory but the fruits of victory; but she it is that sweetens all the spoil. Thus, by a just fate the booty cannot fall to him who did not win it. There is victory in every effort. In the least swing of the arm, an indignant thought, in stern content, we conquer our foes.

❲ One moment of serene and confident life is more glorious than a whole campaign of daring. We should be ready for all issues, not daring to die but daring to live. To the brave even danger is an ally. In their daily life all are braver than they know.

❲ If a man were to place himself in an attitude to bear manfully the greatest evil that can be inflicted on him, he would find suddenly that there was no such evil to bear, his brave back would go a begging.

❲ The coward was born one day too late, for he has never overtaken the present hour. He does not dwell on the earth as though he had a deed of the land in his pocket — not as another lump of nature, as imperturbable an occupant as the stones in the field. He has only rented a few acres of time and space, and thinks that every accident portends the expiration of his lease. He is a non-proprietor, a serf, in his moral economy nomadic, having no fixed abode.

❲ When an Indian is burned, his body may be broiled, it may be no more than a beef-steak. What of that? They may broil his heart, but they do not therefore broil his courage — his principles. Be of good courage! That is the main thing.

❡ The wise gods will never make underpinning of a man. But as long as he crouches, and skulks, and shirks his work, every creature that has weight will be treading on his toes, and crushing him; he will himself tread with one foot on the other foot.

❡ A brave man always knows the way, no matter how intricate the roads.

❡ The only prayer for a brave man is to be a-doing. This is the prayer that is heard. Why ask God for a respite when he has not given it? Has he not done his work, and made man equal to his occasion, but he must have recourse to him again? God cannot give us any other help than self-help.

❡ Fear creates danger, and courage dispels it.

❡ The day is never so dark, nor the night even, but that the laws of light still prevail, and so may make it light in our minds if they are open to the truth. I never yet knew the sun to be knocked down and rolled through a mud puddle; he comes out honor bright from behind every storm.

❡ We should impart our courage, and not our despair; our health and ease, and not our disease; and take care that this does not spread by contagion.

❦ Take time by the forelock. Now or never. You must live in the present, launch yourself on every wave, find your eternity in each moment. Fools stand on their island opportunities and look toward another land. There is no other land; there is no other life but this, or the like of this.

❦ Nothing is so much to be feared as fear. Atheism may comparatively be popular with God himself.

❦ Do not stop to be scared yet; there are more terrible things to come, and ever to come. Men die of fright and live of confidence.

❦ We do all stand in the front ranks of battle every moment of our lives; where there is a brave man there is the thickest of the fight, there the post of honor.

❦ Whatever your sex or position, life is a battle in which you are to show your pluck, and woe be to the coward. Whether passed on a bed of sickness or a tented field, it is ever the same fair play and admits no foolish distinction. Despair and postponement are cowardice and defeat. Men were born to succeed, not to fail.

❦ What a different aspect will courage put upon the face of things.

❨ The monster is never just where we think he is. What is truly monstrous is our cowardice and sloth.

❨ One while we do not wonder that so many commit suicide, life is so barren and worthless; we only live on by an effort of the will. Suddenly our condition is ameliorated, and even the barking of a dog is a pleasure to us. So closely is our happiness bound up with our physical condition, and one reacts on the other.

❨ O for a man who is a *man,* and, as my neighbor says, has a bone in his back which you cannot pass your hand through.

❨ What poor crack-brains we are! easily upset and unable to take care of ourselves. If there were a precipice at our doors, some would be found jumping off today for fear that, if they survived, they might jump off tomorrow.

❨ Do not despair of life. You have no doubt force enough to overcome your obstacles. Think of the fox prowling through wood and field in a winter night for something to satisfy his hunger. Notwithstanding cold and hounds and traps, his race survives. I do not believe any of them ever committed suicide.

34

❡ The winter was not given to us for no purpose. We must thaw its cold with our genialness. We are tasked to find out and appropriate all the nutriment it yields. If it is a cold and hard season, its fruit, no doubt, is the more concentrated and nutty. It took the cold and bleakness of November to ripen the walnut, but the human brain is the kernal which the winter itself matures. Not till then does its shell come off.

❡ To be active, well, happy, implies rare courage. To be ready to fight in a duel implies desperation, or that you hold your life cheap.

❡ The universe expects every man to do his duty in his parallel of latitude.

❡ How can any man be weak who dares *to be* at all?

❡ Even in winter we maintain a temperate cheer and a serene inward life, not destitute of warmth and melody. Only the cold evergreens wear the aspect of summer now and shelter the winter birds.

❡ Keep a stiff fin then, and stem all the tides thou mayest meet.

❧ Sickness should not be allowed to extend further than the body. We need only to retreat further within us to preserve uninterrupted the continuity of serene hours to the end of our lives. As soon as I find my chest is not of tempered steel, and heart of adamant, I bid good-bye to these and look out a new nature. I will be liable to no accidents.

❡ What is the pill which will keep us well, serene, contented? For my panacea let me have a draught of undiluted morning air. Morning air! If men will not drink of this at the fountainhead of the day, why, then, we must even bottle up some and sell it in the shops, for the benefit of those who have lost their subscription ticket to morning time in this world.

❡ You must converse much with the field and woods, if you would imbibe such health into your mind and spirit as you covet for your body.

❡ Surely joy is the condition of life. Think of the young fry that leap in ponds, the myriads of insects ushered into being on a summer evening, the incessant note of the hyla with which the woods ring in the spring, the nonchalance of the butterfly carrying accident and change painted in a thousand hues upon its wings, or the brook minnow stoutly stemming the current, the lustre of whose scales worn bright by the attrition is reflected upon the bank.

❡ Above all, we cannot afford not to live in the present. He is blessed over all mortals who loses no moment of the passing life in remembering the past.

❦ I would keep some book of natural history always by me as a sort of elixir, the reading of which would restore the tone of my system. To him who contemplates a trait of natural beauty no harm nor disappointment can come. The doctrines of despair, of spiritual or political tyranny or servitude, were never taught by such as shared the serenity of nature. The spruce, the hemlock, and the pine, will not countenance despair.

❦ I have noticed that notional nervous invalids, who report to the community the exact condition of their heads and stomachs every morning, as if they alone were blessed or cursed with these parts, who are old betties and quiddles — observe that such are self-indulgent persons, without any regular and absorbing employment. They are nice, discriminating, experienced in all that relates to bodily sensations. They come to you stroking their wens, manipulating their ulcers, and expect you to do the same for them. They spend the day manipulating their bodies and doing no work, they never get their nails clean.

❦ Nothing is so good medicine in sickness as to witness some nobleness in another which will advertise us of health. In sickness it is our faith that ails, and noble deeds reassure us.

❦ Is not disease the rule of existence? There is not a lily pad floating on the river but has been riddled by insects. Almost every shrub and tree has its gall, oftentimes esteemed its chief ornament and hardly to be distinguished from the fruit. If misery loves company, misery has company enough.

❦ The unwise are accustomed to speak as if some were not sick; but methinks the difference between men in respect to health is not great enough to lay much stress upon. Some are reputed sick and some are not. It often happens that the sicker man is the nurse to the sounder.

❦ Disease is not the accident of the individual, nor even of the generation, but of life itself. In some form, and to some degree or other, it is one of the permanent conditions of life. It is, nevertheless, a cheering fact that men affirm health unanimously, and esteem themselves miserable failures. Here was no blunder. They gave us life on exactly these conditions, and methinks we shall live it with more heart when we perceive clearly that these are the terms on which we have it. Life is a warfare, a struggle, and the diseases of the body answer to the troubles and defects of the spirit.

❡ All health and success does me good, however far off and withdrawn it may appear; all disease and failure helps to make me sad and does me evil, however much sympathy it may have with me or I with it. If, then, we would indeed restore mankind by truly Indian, botanic, magnetic, or natural means, let us first be as simple and well as Nature ourselves, dispel the clouds which hang over our own brows, and take up a little life into our pores.

❡ All that a man has to say or do that can possibly concern mankind, is in some shape or other to tell the story of his love — to sing, and, if he is fortunate and keeps alive, he will be forever in love. This alone is to be alive to the extremities. It is a pity that this divine creature should ever suffer from cold feet; a still greater pity that the coldness so often reaches to his heart.

❡ We begin to die, not in our senses or extremities, but in our divine faculties. Our members may be sound, our sight and hearing perfect, but our genius and imagination betray signs of decay. You tell me that you are growing old and troubled to see without glasses, but this is unimportant if the divine faculty of the seer shows no sign of decay.

8. RELAXATION

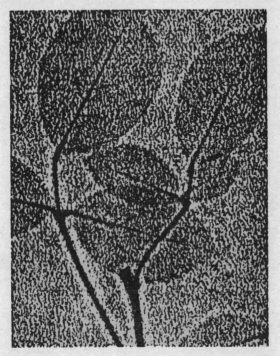

❡ A broad margin of leisure is as beautiful in a man's life as in a book. Haste makes waste, no less in life than in housekeeping. Keep the time, observe the hours of the universe, not of the railroad cars. What are three score years and ten hurriedly and coarsely lived, to moments of divine leisure in which your life is coincident with the life of the universe? We live too fast and coarsely, just as we eat too fast, and do not know the true savor of our food.

⟪When we are unhurried and wise we perceive that only great and worthy things have any permanent and absolute existence — that petty fears and petty pleasures are but the shadow of reality. This is always exhilarating and sublime.

⟪ Let us spend one day as deliberately as Nature, and not be thrown off the track by every nutshell and mosquito's wing that falls on the rail. Let us rise early and fast, or break fast, gently and without perturbation let company come and let company go, let the bells ring and the children cry — determined to make a day of it. Why should we knock under and go with the stream?

⟪ I have frequently seen a poet withdraw, having enjoyed the most valuable part of a farm, while the crusty farmer supposed that he had got a few wild apples only. Why, the owner does not know it for many years when a poet has put his farm in rhyme, the most admirable kind of invisible fence; has fairly impounded it, milked it, skimmed it, and got all the cream, and left the farmer only the skimmed milk.

❦ What if I could pray aloud or to myself as I went along by the brooksides a cheerful prayer like the birds. For joy I could embrace the earth; I shall delight to be buried in it. I sometimes feel as I were rewarded merely for expecting better hours.

❦ Health requires this relaxation, this aimless life. This life in the present.

❦ To be a philosopher is not merely to have subtle thoughts, nor even to found a school, but so to love wisdom as to live according to its dictates, a life of simplicity, independence, magnanimity and trust.

❦ We have lived not in proportion to the number of years that we have spent on the earth, but in proportion as we have enjoyed.

❦ To be calm, to be serene. There is the calmness of the lake when there is not a breath of wind; there is the calmness of a stagnant ditch. So is it with us. Sometimes we are clarified and calmed healthily, as we never were before in our lives, not by an opiate, but by some unconscious obedience to the all-just laws, so that we become like a still lake of purest crystal and without an effort our depths are revealed to ourselves. All the world goes by and is reflected in our deeps.

❦ Nature never makes haste; her systems revolve at an even pace. The buds swell imperceptibly, without hurry or confusion, as though the short spring days were an eternity. Why, then, should man hasten as if anything less than eternity were allotted for the least deed? The wise man is restful, never restless or impatient. He each moment abides where he is, as some walkers actually rest the whole body at each step, while others never relax the muscles of the legs till the accumulated fatigue obliges them to stop short.

❦ Drifting in a sultry day on the sluggish waters of the pond, I almost cease to live and begin to be.

❦ Why should we live with such hurry and waste in life? We are determined to be starved before we are hungry. Men say that a stitch in time saves nine, and so they take a thousand stitches today to save nine tomorrow.

❦ While I bask in the sun on the shores of Walden Pond, by this heat and this rustle, I am absolved from all obligation to the past. The council of nations may reconsider their votes; the grating of a pebble annuls them.

9. RE-CREATION

℄ Live in each season as it passes; breathe the air; drink the drink, taste the fruit, and resign yourself to the influence of each. Let them be your only diet, drink and botanical medicines. Be blown on by all the winds. Open all your pores and bathe in all the tides of nature, in all her streams and oceans, at all seasons.

❡ An early morning walk is a blessing for the whole day.

❡ Our moments of inspiration are not lost though we have no particular poem to show for them; for those experiences have left an indelible impression, and we are ever and anon reminded of them.

❡ I experienced sometimes that the most sweet and tender, the most innocent and encouraging society may be found in any natural object, even for the most melancholy man.

❡ We must be refreshed by the sight of inexhaustible vigor, vast and Titanic features, the sea coast with its wrecks, the wilderness with its living and decayed trees, the thunder cloud, and the rain which lasts three weeks and produces freshets. We need to witness our own limits transgressed, and some life pasturing freely where we never wander.

❡ When I would recreate myself, I seek the darkest wood, the thickest and most interminable, and to the citizen, most dismal swamp. I enter a swamp as a sacred place — a *sanctum sanctorum*. There is the strength, the marrow of nature. The wild-wood covers the virgin mould — and the same soil is good for men and trees.

❡ Take long walks in stormy weather or through deep snows in the fields and woods, if you would keep your spirits up. Deal with brute nature. Be cold and hungry and weary.

❡ He is the man truly — courageous, wise, ingenious — who can use his thoughts and ecstasies as the material of fair and durable creations.

❡ There can be no very black melancholy to him who lives in the midst of Nature and has his senses still. There was never yet such a storm but it was Aeolian music to a healthy and innocent ear. Nothing can rightly compel a simple and brave man to a vulgar sadness. I trust that nothing can make life a burden to me.

❡ You must love the crust of the earth on which you dwell more than the sweet crust of any bread or cake. You must be able to extract nutriment out of a sand-heap. You must have so good an appetite as this, else you will live in vain.

❡ A man dwells in his native valley like a corolla in its calyx, like an acorn in its cup. *Here,* of course, is all that you love, all that you expect, all that you are. Here is your bride elect, as close to you as she can be got.

47

Here is all the best and all the worst you can imagine. What more do you want? Bear her away then! Foolish people imagine that what they imagine is somewhere else. That stuff is not made in any factory but their own.

❦ When I saw the bare sand at Cochituate I felt my relation to the soil. These are *my* sands not yet run out. Not yet will the fates turn the glass. In this clean sand my bones will gladly lie. Like violets I shall be ready to bloom again here in my Indian summer days. Here ever springing, never dying, with perennial root I stand; for the winter of the land is warm to me. While the flowers bloom again as in the spring, shall I pine?

❦ Heaven is under our feet as well as over our heads.

❦ When the common man looks into the sky, which he has not so much profaned, he thinks it less gross than the earth, and with reverence speaks of "the Heavens," but the seer will in the same sense speak of "the Earths," and his Father who is in them.

❦ Of thee, O earth, are my bone and sinew made: to thee, O sun, am I brother. Here have I my habitat. I am of thee.

10. HUMAN FAITH

❡ That we have but little faith is not sad, but that we have little faithfulness. By faithfulness faith is earned.

❡ Men of little faith stand only by their feet— or recline on the ground, having lost their reliance on the soul.

❡ In view of the future or possible, we should live quite laxly and undefined in front, our outlines dim and misty on that side; as our shadows reveal an insensible perspiration toward the sun.

❡ One of little faith looks for his rewards and punishments to the next world, and, despairing of this world, behaves accordingly in it; another thinks the present a worthy occasion and arena, sacrifices to it, and expects to hear sympathizing voices. The man who believes in another world and not in this is wont to put me off with Christianity. The present world in which we talk is of a little less value to him than the next world. So we are said to hope in proportion as we do not realize. It is all hope deferred. But one grain of realization, of instant life, on which we stand, is equivalent to acres of hope hammered out to gild our prospect.

❡ We are older by faith than by experience.

❡ We must have infinite faith in each other. If we have not, we must never let it leak out that we have not....When I hear a grown man or woman say, "Once I had faith in men, now I have not," I am inclined to ask, "Who are you whom the world has disappointed? Have not you rather disappointed the world? There is the same ground for faith now that ever there was: It needs only a little love in you who complain so to ground it on." The mason asks but a narrow shelf to spring his brick from; man requires only an infinitely narrower one to spring the arch of faith from.

❡ Though I should put up a [lightning] rod if its utility were satisfactorily demonstrated to me, yet, so mixed are we, I should feel myself safe or in danger quite independently of the senseless rod. Yet there is a degree of faith and righteousness in putting up a rod, as well as trusting without one, though the latter, which is the rarest, I feel to be the most effectual rod of the two.

❡ How serenity, anxiety, confidence, fear, paint the heavens for us.

❡ Again I scent the white water-lily, and a season I had waited for is arrived. It is the emblem of purity and its scent suggests it. Growing in stagnant and muddy water, it bursts up so pure and fair to the eye and so sweet to the scent, as if to show us what purity and sweetness reside in, and can be extracted from, the slime and muck of earth. What confirmation of our hopes is in the fragrance of the water-lily! I shall not so soon despair of the world for it.

❦ What a consolation are the stars to man! — so high and out of his reach. I do not know but my life is fated to be thus low and groveling always. I cannot discover its use even to myself. But it is permitted to see those stars in the sky equally useless, yet highest of all and deserving of a fair destiny. My fate is in some sense linked with that of the stars, and if they are to preserve to a great end, shall I die who could conjecture it?

❦ Every part of nature teaches that the passing away of one life is the making of room for another. The oak dies down to the ground, leaving within its rind a virgin mould, which will impart a vigorous life to an infant forest.

❦ So our human life but dies down to its root, and still puts forth its green blade to eternity.

❦ What right have I to grieve [over my Brother John's death], who have not ceased to wonder. We feel at first as if some opportunities of kindness and sympathy were lost, but learn afterward that any *pure grief* is ample recompense for all. Soon the ice will melt, and the blackbirds sing, along the river which he frequented, as pleasantly as ever. The same everlasting serenity will appear in this face of God, and we will not be sorrowful, if He is not.

❡ Nature refuses to sympathize with our sorrow. She seems not to have provided for, but by a thousand contrivances, against it. She has beveled the margins of the eyelids that the tears may not overflow on the cheek.

❡ On the death of a friend, we should consider that the fates through confidence have devolved on us the task of a double living, that we have henceforth to fulfill the promise of our friend's life also, in our own, to the world.

❡ Everyone has heard the story which has gone the rounds of New England, of a strong and beautiful bug which came out of the dry leaf of an old table of apple-tree wood, which had stood in the farmer's kitchen for sixty years, first in Connecticut, and afterward in Massachusetts — from an egg deposited in the living tree many years earlier, as appeared by counting the annual layers beyond it — which was heard gnawing out for several weeks, hatched perchance by the heat of an urn. Who does not feel his faith in a resurrection and immortality strengthened by hearing this?

❡ The delicious soft, spring-suggesting air — how it fills my veins with life! Life becomes again credible to me. A certain dormant life awakes in me and I begin to love nature again.

❧ I thank God for sorrow. It is hard to be abused. Is not He kind still, who lets this south wind blow, this warm sun shine on me?

❧ You ask if there is no doctrine of sorrow in my philosophy. Of acute sorrow I suppose that I know comparatively little. My saddest and most genuine sorrows are apt to be but transient regrets. The place of sorrow is supplied, perchance, by a certain hard and proportionably barren indifference. I am kin to the sod and partake largely of its dull patience — in winter expecting the sun of spring.

❧ If you are afflicted with melancholy at this season [October], go to the swamp and see the brave spears of the skunk cabbage already advanced toward a new year. Their gravestones are not bespoken yet. Who shall be sexton to them? Is it the winter of their discontent? Do they seem to have lain down to die, despairing of skunk cabbagedom?

❧ Alas! this is the crying sin of the age, this want of faith in the prevalence of a man. Nothing can be affected but by one man. He who wants help wants everything. True, this is the condition of our weakness, but it can never be the means of recovery. We must first succeed alone, that we may enjoy our success together.

11. THE GREAT SPIRIT

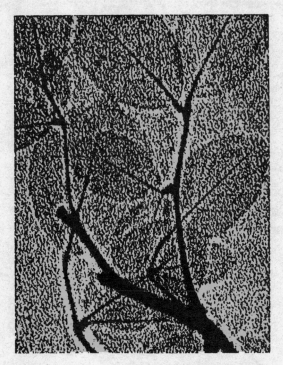

ℂ When we would rest our bodies we cease to support them; we recline on the lap of earth. So when we would rest our spirits, we must recline on the Great Spirit.

℃ If by watching all day and all night I may detect some trace of the Ineffable, then will it not be worth the while to watch?

❡ We have had a succession of thunder-showers today and at sunset a rainbow. . . . After the rain He sets his bow in the heavens! The world is not destitute of beauty. Ask of the skeptic who inquires, *Cui bono?* why the rainbow was made. While men cultivate flowers below, God cultivates flowers above; He takes charge of the parterres in the heavens. Is not the rainbow a faint vision of God's face? How glorious should be the life of man passed under this arch!

❡ My desire for knowledge is intermittent; but my desire to commune with the spirit of the universe, to be intoxicated with the fumes, call it, of the divine nectar, to bear my head through atmospheres and over heights unknown to my feet, is perennial and constant.

❡ The bigoted and sectarian forget that without religion or devotion of some kind nothing great was ever accomplished.

❡ Truly, our greatest blessings are very cheap.

❡ The ears were made, not for such trivial uses as men are wont to suppose, but to hear celestial sounds. The eyes were not made for such groveling uses as they are now put to and worn out by, but to behold beauty now invisible. May we not *see* God?

❡ My profession is to be always on the alert to find God in nature, to know His lurking places, to attend all the oratories, the operas, in Nature. To watch for, describe, all the divine features which I detect in Nature.

❡ We can only live healthily the life the gods assign us. I must receive my life as passively as the willow leaf that flutters over the brook. I must not be for myself, but God's work, and that is always good. I will wait the breezes patiently, and grow as they shall determine. My fate cannot but be grand so. We may live the life of a plant or animal without living an animal life. This constant and universal content of the animal comes of resting quietly in God's palm. I feel as if I could at any time resign my life and the responsibility into God's hands and become as innocent and free from care as a plant or stone.

❡ The gods are of no sect; they side with no man. When I imagine that Nature inclined rather to some few earnest and faithful souls, and specially existed for them, I go to see an obscure individual who lives under the hill, letting both gods and men alone, and find that strawberries and tomatoes grow for him too in his garden there, and the sun lodges kindly under his hillside, and am compelled to acknowledge the unbribable charity of the gods.

℄ There are various, nay, incredible faiths: why should we be alarmed at any of them? What man believes, God believes.

℄ God did not make this world in jest; no, nor in indifference.

℄ The great God is very calm withal. How superfluous is any excitement in His creatures! He listens equally to the prayers of the believer and unbeliever. The moods of man should unfold and alternate as gradually as those of nature. The sun shines for aye! The sudden revolutions of these times and this generation have acquired a very exaggerated importance. They do not interest me much, for they are not in harmony with the longer periods of nature. The present, in any aspect in which it can be presented to the smallest audience, is always mean. God does not sympathize with the popular movements.

℄ In most men's religion the ligature which should be its muscle and sinew is rather like that thread which the accomplices of Cylon held in their hands, when they went abroad from the temple of Minerva, the other end being attached to the statue of the goddess. But frequently, as in their case, the thread breaks, being stretched, and they are left without an asylum.

❡ As my own hand bent aside the willow in my path, so must my single arm put to flight the devil and his angels. God is not our ally when we shrink, and neuter when we are bold. If by trusting in God you lose any part of your vigor, trust in Him no longer. When you trust, do not lay aside your armor, put it on and buckle it tighter.

❡ In eternity there is indeed something true and sublime. But all these times and places and occasions are now and here. God himself culminates in the present moment, and will never be more divine in the lapse of all the ages. And we are enabled to apprehend at all what is sublime and noble only by the perpetual instilling and drenching of the reality that surrounds us.

❡ I delight to come to my bearings — not walk in procession with pomp and parade, in a conspicuous place, but to walk even with the Builder of the universe, if I may — not to live in this restless, nervous, bustling, trivial Nineteenth Century, but stand or sit thoughtfully while it goes by.

❡ Men obey their call and go to the stove-warmed church, though God exhibits himself to the walker in a frosted bush today as much as in a burning one to Moses of old.

❡ The Great Spirit makes indifferent all times and places. The place where he is seen is always the same, and indescribably pleasant to all our senses. We had allowed only neighboring and transient circumstances to make our occasions. They were, in fact, the causes of our distraction. But nearest to all things is that power which fashions their being.

❡ Next to us the grandest laws are being enacted and administered. Next to us is not the workman whom we have hired, but ever the workman whose work we are. He is at work, not in my backyard, but inconceivably nearer than that. We are the subjects of an experiment how singular? Can we not dispense with the society of our gossips a little while under these circumstances?

❡ As I stand over the insect crawling amid the pine needles on the forest floor, and endeavoring to conceal itself from my sight, and ask myself why it will cherish these humble thoughts, and hide its head from me who might, perhaps, be its benefactor, and impart to its race some cheering information, I am reminded of the greater Benefactor and Intelligence that stands over me the human insect.

❡ Be of good cheer. Those Jews were too sad; to another people a still deeper revelation may suggest only joy. Don't I know what gladness is? Is it but the reflex of sadness, its back side? In the Hebrew gladness, I hear but too distinctly still the sound of sadness retreating. Give me a gladness which has never given place to sadness.

℄ If we are not blind, we shall see how a right hand is stretched over all, as well the unlucky as lucky, and that the ordering soul is only right-handed, distributing with one palm all our fates.

℄ There is something proudly thrilling in the thought that this obedience to conscience and trust in God, which is so solemnly preached in extremities and arduous circumstances, is only to retreat to one's self, and rely on our own strength. In trivial circumstances I find myself sufficient to myself, and in the most momentous I have no ally but myself, and must silently put by their harm by my own strength, as I did the former.

℄ I know that I am. I know that another is who knows more than I, who takes an interest in me, whose creature, and yet whose kindred in one sense, am I. I know that the enterprise is worthy. I know that things work well. I have heard no bad news.

The editor is indebted to Houghton Mifflin Company for permission to print the material in this book which comes from various titles published by them, and is indebted to Mrs. Ruth B. Robertson for advice and assistance in its compilation.